Word Problems:
120 Math Problems For Kids

Math Workbook Grade 3

Math For Kids Volume 3

By
Stephen Hill

Copyright © 2016 by Wiq Media

ALL RIGHTS RESERVED

No part of this book may be reproduced, stored in a retrieval system, or transmitted in any form or by any means, electronic, mechanical, photocopying, recording, scanning, or otherwise, without the prior written permission of the publisher.

Disclaimer

This Grade 3 math workbook is a resource for practice solving word problems using mathematical operational skills. The ability to read a math problem, devise a strategy, and apply a strategy to solve the problem is a valuable skill that every math student should set as a goal to master. This math for kids book is a tool for supplementing classroom instruction. Regular practice of problem solving skills along with computational skills to attain procedural fluency is recommended. Consistency is the key for student success.

Note To Teachers And Parents

This book can be completed by working one chapter at a time, starting with Chapter 1. Plan on working on a schedule such as daily, weekly, bi-weekly, etc. Have the student work in a distraction-free environment with an adequate workspace. Provide enough space either in the workbook or with additional paper for students to write out key information and devise problem solving strategies. Utilize visual aids such as number lines and hundreds charts if needed. Encourage students to thoroughly read the problem and look for key words that help devise operational strategies. Refer to the answer key only after completing a chapter. Have an adult/parent/tutor/teacher review the problems. If the answers are incorrect, encourage students to review the problem and look for computational errors or operational errors. Maintain a positive attitude that mistakes are part of the journey towards learning and concept/skill mastery. That is why pencils have erasers! If the problems are correct, then move on to the next chapter.

Contents

THE PROBLEMS 1

Chapter 1: Multiplication 2

Chapter 2: Division 5

Chapter 3: Place Value 8

Chapter 4: Adding/Subtracting Multiples of Ten 11

Chapter 5: Write and Solve Two Step Problems? 14

Chapter 6: Area 17

Chapter 7: Perimeter 20

Chapter 8: Money 23

Chapter 9: Elapsed Time 26

Chapter 10: Addition/Subtraction Interpreting a Chart 29

Chapter 11: Multiplication/Measurement 32

Chapter 12: Rounding and Problem Solving 35

Answers Chapter 1 38

Answers Chapter 2 39

Answers Chapter 3 40

Answers Chapter 4 41

Answers Chapter 5 42

Answers Chapter 6 43

Answers Chapter 7 44

Answers Chapter 8 45

Answers Chapter 9 46

Answers Chapter 10 47

Answers Chapter 11 48

Answers Chapter 12 49

One Last Note 50

THE PROBLEMS

There are 12 sections of problems to solve in this book.

Each section contains 10 problems.

That's a total of 120 fun and exciting problems, some are easy, some are harder.

Have fun solving these math problems. Take your time and write down what you are thinking and it will be easier.

Have fun!

Chapter 1:
Multiplication

1. Justin has 3 boxes of baseballs. Each box has 8 baseballs. How many baseballs does Justin have in all?

2. Jess drew a picture of 4 beehives. In each beehive she drew 5 bees. How many bees did Jess draw in all?

3. There are 2 bowls of apples. Each bowl has 9 apples. How many apples are there in all?

4. Kayla's mom bought 5 juice packs. There are 8 juice boxes in each pack. How many total juice boxes did Kayla's mom buy?

5. Manny has 4 candy bars. He broke each candy bar apart into 6 equal pieces. How many equal pieces of candy are there?

6. There are 9 canoes in the river. In each canoe there are 7 people. How many total people are in the canoes?

7. Bo read a story about elves that lived in trees. In each of 5 trees there were 7 elves. How many total elves were in the story that Bo read?

8. The students were placed in 6 groups of 9. How many students were placed in groups?

9. Jim's dad is buying some hooks. He need 7 hooks for each of 4 shelves. How many hooks does Jim's dad need to buy?

10. Lucy put 9 beads on each of 3 necklaces. How many beads did Lucy put on all of the necklaces?

Chapter 2:
Division

1. Tyler has a total of 25 pictures of 5 different insects. He has the same number of each kind of insect. How many pictures of each insect does Tyler have?

2. Mr. Myers wants to put 18 candles in boxes. He wants to put 6 candles in each box. How many boxes does Mr. Myers need for the candles?

3. Terry wants to put 32 potatoes into 4 bags. She wants to put the same number in each bag. How many potatoes should go into each bag?

4. The students put 49 chairs in rows. There are 7 chairs in each row. How many rows of chairs are there?

5. Tina made 56 cookies to put into bags. Tina wants to put 8 cookies in each bag. How many bags does Tina need?

6. Mr. Wilson is passing out 42 crayons to 7 students. He wants to give each student the same number of crayons. How many crayons should each student get?

7. There are 45 band members marching in 5 equal sized rows. How many band members are marching in each row?

8. There are 36 tires for sale. They are sold in packs of 4. How many packs of tires are for sale?

9. Mr. Simon is putting 72 dishes on 8 shelves. He wants to put the same number on each shelf. How many dishes can be put on each shelf?

10. There are 64 basketball players on 8 teams. If the teams are equal, how many players are on each team?

Chapter 3:
Place Value

1. What number is 3 thousands, 6 hundreds, 9 tens and 7 ones?

2. What number is 8 hundreds, 1 thousand, 5 ones and 7 tens?

3. What number is 3 thousands, 4 tens and 4 ones?

4. What number is 2 hundreds, 5 thousands, and 2 ones?

5. What number is 6 tens, 7 hundreds and 4 thousands?

6. What number is 9 tens, 3 ones, 6 thousands and 8 hundreds?

7. What number is 4 ones and 9 thousands?

8. What number is 3 hundreds, 7 ones and 2 thousands?

9. What number is 8 ones, 6 hundreds and 7 thousands?

10. What number is 1 ten, 8 thousands and 2 ones?

Chapter 4:
Adding/Subtracting Multiples of Ten

1. What number is 110 more than 887?

2. What number is 1,001 less than 3,456?

3. What number is 101 more than 7,308?

4. What number is 1,010 less than 6,990?

5. What number is 1,100 more than 5,005?

6. What number is 1,011 less than 3,333?

7. What number is 1,101 more than 4,620?

8. What number is 1,110 less than 2,964?

9. What number is 111 more than 1,832?

10. What number is 111 less than 9,876?

Chapter 5:
Write and Solve Two Step Problems?

1. In the classroom there are 3 rows, each with 7 desks, and 4 extra desks. What is the total number of desks in the classroom?

2. Chris has 2 nickels and 7 pennies. How many total cents does Chris have?

3. Tony and his family are going away for 2 weeks and 5 days. There are 7 days in 1 week. What is the total number of days that Tony and his family are going away?

4. A box of cookies had 9 rows of 9 cookies. Dan and his friends ate 10 cookies. How many cookies are left in the box?

5. In the yard there are 3 tables, each with 4 chairs. There are 2 extra chairs. How many total chairs are in the yard?

6. At the store there are 53 teddy bears. After 5 were sold, the rest were put in 6 baskets with the same number in each basket. How many teddy bears were put in each basket?

7. The 22 students in grade 2 and the 23 students in grade 3 are going on some boat rides. Each boat can hold 5 students. How many boats are needed for all of the students?

8. Some girls are putting balloons in bunches. Each bunch has 6 blue balloons and 4 red balloons in each bunch. How many total balloons are needed for 8 bunches?

9. On the wall there are 4 pictures in each of 4 rows. There are 3 more pictures below the 4 rows. How many total pictures are on the wall?

10. Nick had 33 baseball cards. He gave 3 cards to his brother. The rest of the cards were put in a book. He put 6 cards on each page. How many pages did Nick use for the rest of his baseball cards?

Chapter 6:

Area

1. Miss Porter has a bulletin board in her classroom. The length is 4 feet and the width is 2 feet. What is the area of the bulletin board?

2. Amy's yard has a length of 8 meters and a width of 3 meters. What is the area of Amy's yard?

3. The area of a picture is 63 square inches. The length is 9 inches. What is the width of the picture?

4. Bill has a rug in his room. The length is 5 feet and the width is 3 feet. What is the area of Bill's rug?

5. The area of the rectangle-shaped park is 36 square kilometers. The length is 9 kilometers. What is the width of the park?

6. Ken drew a square with side lengths of 6 centimeters. He wants to cover the square with square centimeter tiles with no gaps or overlaps. How many tiles will Ken need?

7. Lisa has 30 square inch tiles. She wants to make a rectangle. What could be a length and width of the rectangle?

8. There are 18 square feet carpet tiles to use to cover the hallway floor without gaps or overlaps. What could be the length and width of the hallway floor?

9. Rob has 14 square centimeter tiles. He wants to arrange them in a rectangle without gaps or overlaps. What should be the length and width of the square?

10. Kate has 36 square inch tiles. She wants to arrange them in a square. What should be the length and width of the square?

Chapter 7:

Perimeter

1. The length of a picture frame is 7 inches and the width is 5 inches. What is the perimeter of the picture frame?

2. A rectangle has a length of 6 centimeters and a width of 4 centimeters. What is the perimeter of the rectangle?

3. Luke drew a square with side lengths of 8 inches. What is the perimeter of Luke's square?

4. The board in Kyle's classroom has a length of 3 meters and a width of 1 meter. Kyle wants to put a border around the outside of the board without gaps or overlaps. How many meters of border does Kyle need?

5. Ben is putting a ribbon around a picture frame with a length of 10 centimeters and a width of 5 centimeters. How many centimeters of ribbon does Ben need?

6. The kitchen floor has a length of 11 feet and a width of 9 feet. What is the perimeter of the kitchen floor?

7. The perimeter of a rectangle is 20 inches. The length is 6 inches. What is the width?

8. The perimeter of a square is 20 inches. What are the side lengths?

9. The perimeter of a rectangular table top is 16 feet. What could be the length and width?

10. The area of a square is 9 square feet. What is the perimeter of the square?

Chapter 8:
Money

1. How much money is 3 dollars, 3 quarters and 3 nickels?

2. How much money is 4 dollars, 5 dimes and 6 pennies?

3. How much money is 2 dollars, 2 quarters and 4 nickels?

4. How much money is 5 quarters, 2 dimes and 3 pennies?

5. How much money is 1 dollar, 1 quarter, 3 dimes and 3 nickels?

6. How much money is 6 quarters, 3 nickels and 1 penny?

7. How much money is 4 dollars, 2 quarters and 2 nickels?

8. How much money is 2 dollars, 5 quarters and 5 nickels?

9. How much money is 3 dollars, 4 dimes and 4 pennies?

10. How much money is 5 dollars, 4 quarters, 3 dimes, 2 nickels and 1 penny?

Chapter 9:
Elapsed Time

1. How many minutes have passed from 4:05 am to 4:40 am?

2. How many minutes have passed from 2:50 pm to 3:10 pm?

3. How many minutes have passed from 7:10 am to 7:35 am?

4. How many minutes have passed from 6:45 pm to 7:05 pm?

5. How many minutes have passed from 12:35 am to 1:00 am?

6. How many minutes have passed from 5:15 pm to 5:50 pm?

7. How many minutes have passed from 3:40 am to 4:25 am?

8. How many minutes have passed from 11:30 am to 12:25 pm?

9. How many minutes have passed from 9:25 am to 10:15 am?

10. How many minutes have passed from 1:15 pm to 1:55 pm?

Chapter 10:
Addition/Subtraction Interpreting a Chart

The table shows the number of people that visited the zoo for 5 days. Use the information to answer questions 1-10.

Day	Monday	Tuesday	Wednesday	Thursday	Friday
Number of People	415	386	367	509	624

1. How many total people visited the zoo on Monday and Tuesday?

2. How many total people visited the zoo on Wednesday and Thursday?

3. How many total people visited the zoo on Wednesday and Friday?

4. How many total people visited the zoo on Monday and Wednesday?

5. 5. How many total people visited the zoo on Tuesday and Thursday?

6. How many more people visited the zoo on Monday than on Tuesday?

7. How many more people visited the zoo on Tuesday than on Wednesday?

8. How many more people visited the zoo on Thursday than on Wednesday?

9. How many more people visited the zoo on Friday than on Thursday?

10. How many more people visited the zoo on the most visited day and the least visited day?

Chapter 11:
Multiplication/Measurement

1. One yard equals 3 feet. How many feet are equal to 10 yards?

2. One full bottle has 2 liters of water. How many liters are in 30 full bottles?

3. One piece of a fence has a length of 3 meters. What is the total length, in meters, of 50 pieces of the fence?

4. One board has a length of 80 centimeters. What is the total length of 5 boards?

5. One full box of books has a weight of 9 pounds. What is the total weight, in pounds, of 40 full boxes of books?

6. One full barrel holds 20 gallons of water. How many gallons are in 5 full barrels of water?

7. One shirt has a price of $20. What is the price of 6 shirts?

8. One full box of cookies has 80 cookies. How many cookies are in 6 full boxes?

9. One box of cookies has a price of $3. What is the price of 30 boxes of cookies?

10. One piece of ribbon has a length of 8 inches. What is the total length of 40 ribbons?

Chapter 12:
Rounding and Problem Solving

The table shows the number and subject of the books in the school book room. Use the information to answer questions 1-10. Round the numbers to the nearest hundred then solve the problems finding the estimated answer.

Subject	Math	Science	Reading	Social Studies	Spelling
Number of Books	681	649	755	519	443

1. About how many Math and Science books are there in all?

2. About how many Science and Reading books are there in all?

3. About how many Reading and Social Studies books are there in all?

4. About how many Science and Social Studies books are there in all?

5. About how many Reading and Spelling books are there in all?

6. About how many more Math books are there than Social Studies books?

7. About how many more Reading books are there than Science books?

8. About how many more Science books are there than Spelling books?

9. About how many more Math books are there than Spelling books?

10. About how many more Math and Science books are there than Social Studies and Spelling books?

Answers Chapter 1

1. 24 baseballs
2. 20 bees
3. 18 apples
4. 40 juice boxes
5. 24 equal pieces
6. 63 people
7. 35 elves
8. 54 students
9. 28 hooks
10. 27 beads

Answers Chapter 2

1. 5 pictures
2. 3 boxes
3. 8 potatoes
4. 7 rows
5. 8 bags
6. 6 crayons
7. 9 band members
8. 9 packs
9. 9 dishes
10. 8 players

Answers Chapter 3

1. 3,697
2. 1,875
3. 3,044
4. 5,201
5. 4,760
6. 6,893
7. 9,004
8. 2,307
9. 7,608
10. 8,012

Answers Chapter 4

1. 997
2. 2,455
3. 7,409
4. 5,980
5. 6,105
6. 2,322
7. 5,727
8. 1,854
9. 1,943
10. 9,765

Answers Chapter 5

1. 25 desks
2. 17 cents
3. 19 days
4. 71 cookies
5. 14 chairs
6. 8 teddy bears
7. 9 boats
8. 80 balloons
9. 19 pictures
10. 5 pages

Answers Chapter 6

1. 8 square feet
2. 24 square yards
3. 7 inches
4. 15 square feet
5. 4 kilometers
6. 36 square centimeter tiles
7. 3 inches and 10 inches; or 6 inches and 5 inches; or 2 inches and 15 inches
8. 9 feet and 2 feet; or 3 feet and 6 feet; or 18 feet and 1 foot
9. 2 centimeters and 7 centimeters
10. 6 inches

Answers Chapter 7

1. 24 inches
2. 20 centimeters
3. 32 inches
4. 8 meters
5. 30 centimeters
6. 40 feet
7. 4 inches
8. 5 inches
9. 6 feet and 2 feet; or 5 feet and 3 feet; or 7 feet and 1 foot; or 4 feet (a square can be classified as a rectangle)
10. 12 feet

Answers Chapter 8

1. $3.90
2. $4.56
3. $2.70
4. $1.48
5. $1.70
6. $1.66
7. $4.60
8. $3.50
9. $3.44
10. $6.41

Answers Chapter 9

1. 35 minutes
2. 20 minutes
3. 25 minutes
4. 20 minutes
5. 25 minutes
6. 35 minutes
7. 45 minutes
8. 55 minutes
9. 50 minutes
10. 40 minutes

Answers Chapter 10

1. 801 people
2. 876 people
3. 991 people
4. 782 people
5. 895 people
6. 29 people
7. 19 people
8. 142 people
9. 115 people
10. 257 people

Answers Chapter 11

1. 30 feet
2. 60 liters
3. 150 meters
4. 400 centimeters
5. 360 pounds
6. 100 gallons
7. $120
8. 480 cookies
9. $90
10. 320 inches

Answers Chapter 12

1. 1,300
2. 1.400
3. 1.300
4. 1,100
5. 1,200
6. 200
7. 200
8. 200
9. 300
10. 400

One Last Note

Thanks for going through this book of math problems. You're now smarter than what you were before you started the book, congratulations! If you liked the book and want to see more books like this, please check out all of our Math books on Amazon.

Also, if you would be so kind to leave a review of this book, we would be very grateful.

Made in the USA
Las Vegas, NV
15 December 2023